Carousel Animals
Coloring Book

Christy Shaffer

DOVER PUBLICATIONS, INC.
Mineola, New York

Introduction

The carousel, American as apple pie, is descended from a war game played by Turkish and Arabian horsemen in the 12th century. Introduced into France in the late 13th century, the carousel evolved into an equestrian fete, including a tournament in which riders attempted to spear a ring hanging between posts. By the late 17th century, French horsemen were practicing for this event on crude wooden horses suspended from beams rotating around a center pole. The massive wheel was pushed by servants or animals. The English attached the steam engine in the 19th century, giving birth to the carousel as we know it.

In the late 1800s, European immigrants skilled in carving and building carousels arrived in the United States. With the American economy on the upswing, owners of newly completed trolley lines installed amusement parks at the ends of the tracks as a way to increase revenue. Hordes of people, now able to travel inexpensively, flocked to these attractions where they discovered the delights of carousel riding. The merry-go-round, with its fanciful, painted ponies, became a symbol of America, the land of opportunity. Soaring profits spurred fierce competition among the carousel manufacturers, raising the level of carousel design to unsurpassed heights of glitter and grandeur.

Between 1900 and 1925, European-trained carvers created more than 4,000 carousels in the United States. Today, as a result of fires, floods, and neglect, fewer than 170 remain. Surviving carousels and pieces of carousels, now revered as American folk art, are owned by municipalities, amusement parks, art institutions, carousel museums, and private collectors. Carousel associations have been established across the country to help preserve these splendid machines.

The carousel animals portrayed on the following pages have been drawn to depict the styles of America's finest carousel carvers. As you bring them to life with the addition of color, may they remind you of the innocence and wonder of days gone by.

Bibliographical Note

Carousel Animals Coloring Book is a new work, first published by Dover Publications, Inc., in 1999.

International Standard Book Number
ISBN-13: 978-0-486-40804-0
ISBN-10: 0-486-40804-3

Manufactured in the United States by Courier Corporation
40804311   2013
www.doverpublications.com

The lead horse, or king horse, was the most elaborately carved and decorated figure on the carousel. Horses decked in armor were most popular.

This lead horse wears ornamental trappings in the style of carver Marcus Illions. Eye-catching decorations were designed to entice customers.

Carousel animals were created in three poses: standing, prancing, and jumping. Standing animals, placed on the outside row of the carousel, provided stability for riders questing for the brass ring which would earn them a free ride.

With its two back legs resting on the carousel platform, and its front legs rearing into the air, this prancing Indian pony would probably be placed in the second row.

This Art Nouveau-style jumper, with four feet off the ground, moves up and down on a pole as the carousel revolves. It is illustrated in the style of carver Daniel Muller.

The viewing, or romance side of a carousel horse, was carved with fanciful trappings and flowing manes. It glittered with brightly colored paint and glass jewels.

The carving of elaborate trappings was labor-intensive and expensive. The inner, or non-romance side of a horse, shown here, was sparely carved, since it was rarely seen.

The style of Stein and Goldstein was to create fierce-looking Trojan horses with cropped manes, roman noses, large buckles, and deeply carved ornamentation.

The head of this horse, drawn in the style of Coney Island carver Charles Carmel, shows two of his signature details: a flowing mane and an extended tongue.

Mexican carver Luis Ortega was revered for his horses with flamboyantly carved and painted manes that resembled Aztec headdresses. The horses were often posed with their necks twisted back, which created a powerful, menacing appearance.

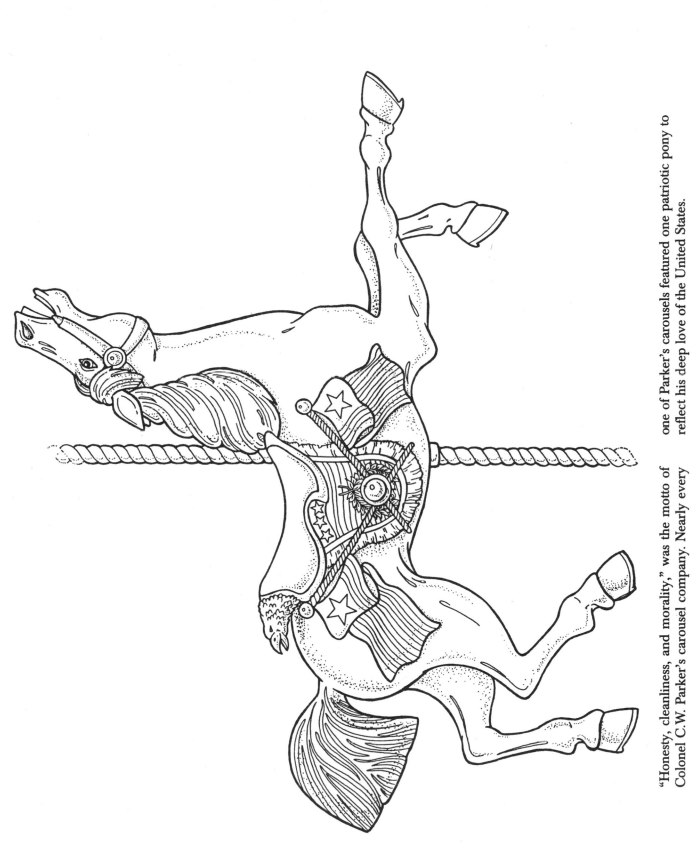

"Honesty, cleanliness, and morality," was the motto of Colonel C.W. Parker's carousel company. Nearly every one of Parker's carousels featured one patriotic pony to reflect his deep love of the United States.

Herschell-Spillman's plainly carved ponies were used for one-night engagements at carnivals and country fairs. Their compact, unadorned bodies were relatively easy to pack, transport, and set up.

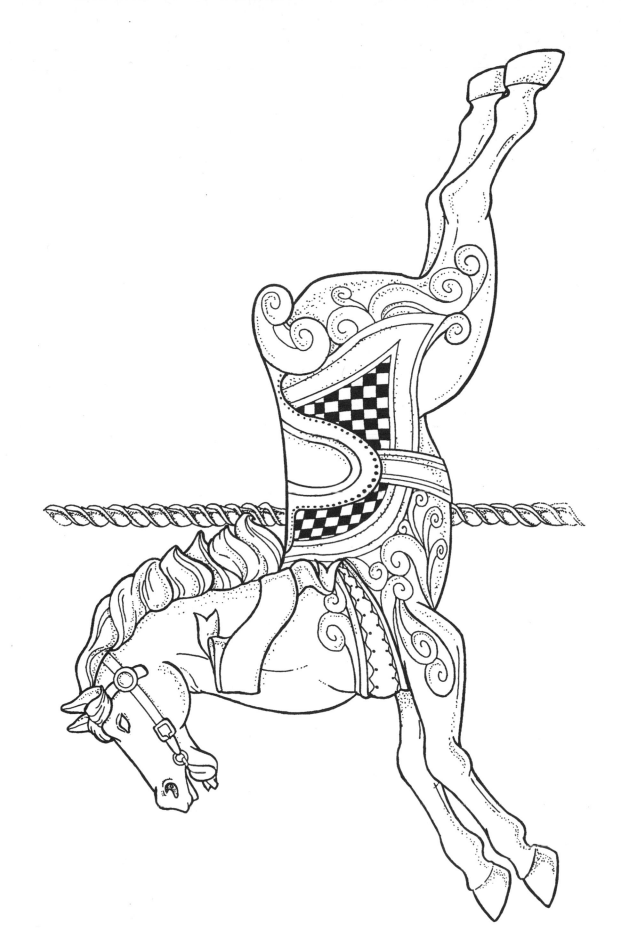

"Gallopers," or British carousel ponies, rotate counter clockwise so that the romance side is on the animals' left. These ponies generally feature banners on their necks which carry their names. The banner on the pony here is blank so that you may name it.

The popular amusement park ride that featured a revolving platform and carved wooden ponies, or other creatures, is known by many names: carousel, flying horses, whirligig, flying jinny, steam circus, riding gallery, carry-us-all, and merry-go-round.

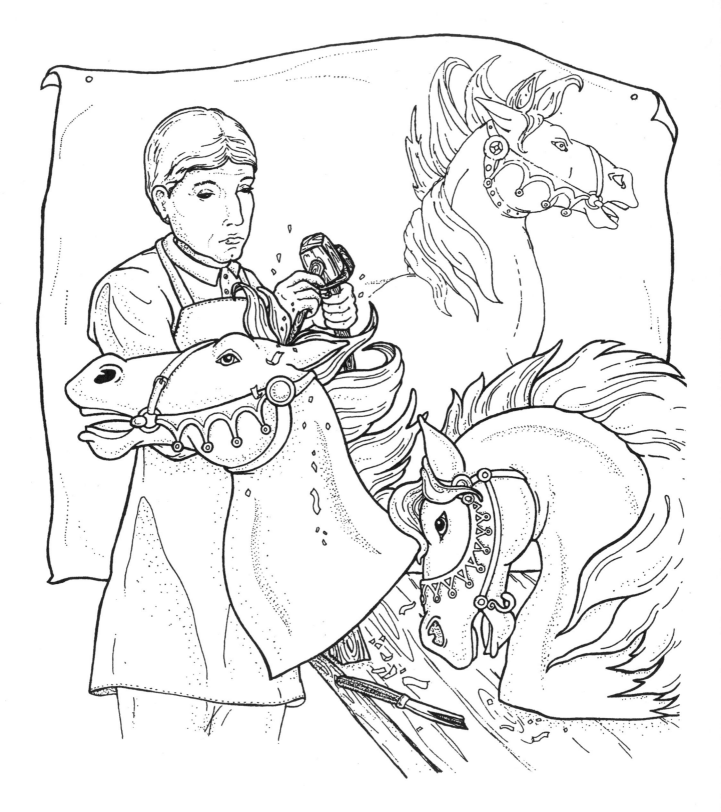

Carvers could copy the prototype of a pony in less than 40 hours. So skilled were they at their craft, and so precise were the renderings, that replications appeared to be identical to the original. The most talented carver of a team created the animal's head, inspiring the term, "head man."

This magnificent Dentzel-style lion is characterized by powerful muscles, royal trappings, and a regal demeanor. Lions were among the first animals, other than horses, to be portrayed on carousels.

Charles I.D. Looff's exotic menagerie of carved beasts launched the popularity of carousel animals beyond horses. Perhaps it was the gentle, whimsical expression of the creatures, as depicted in this giraffe, drawn in the Looff style, that made his animals so appealing.

Looff carved fifty-four animals as a wedding gift for his daughter, Emma. These were among the last of Looff's works before he retired. The carousel beast shown here, depicted in Looff's style, portrays "Sneaky" the tiger in an unusual prowling or stalking pose.

Designed without caparisons, or ornamental covering, this striking Herschell-Spillman-like zebra exudes the aura of unbridled freedom. To enhance the look of a wild, untamed animal, the finished piece (this one shown from the non-romance side) relies more on the painter's skill than on the carver's trappings.

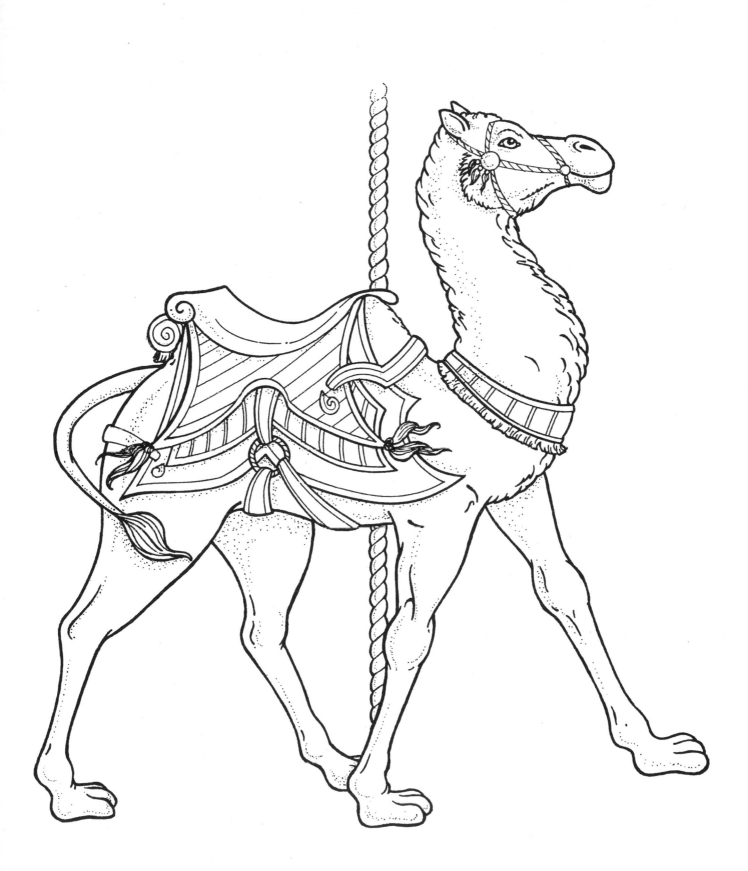

This drawing shows detailed carvings in the style of E. Joy Morris, including an intricately woven harness strap and a fancy saddle.

Many carousels were created around romantic fantasy themes such as the medieval era, or the Arabian nights.

Other styles were festive and patriotic. This Dentzel-inspired goat reflects a circus motif.

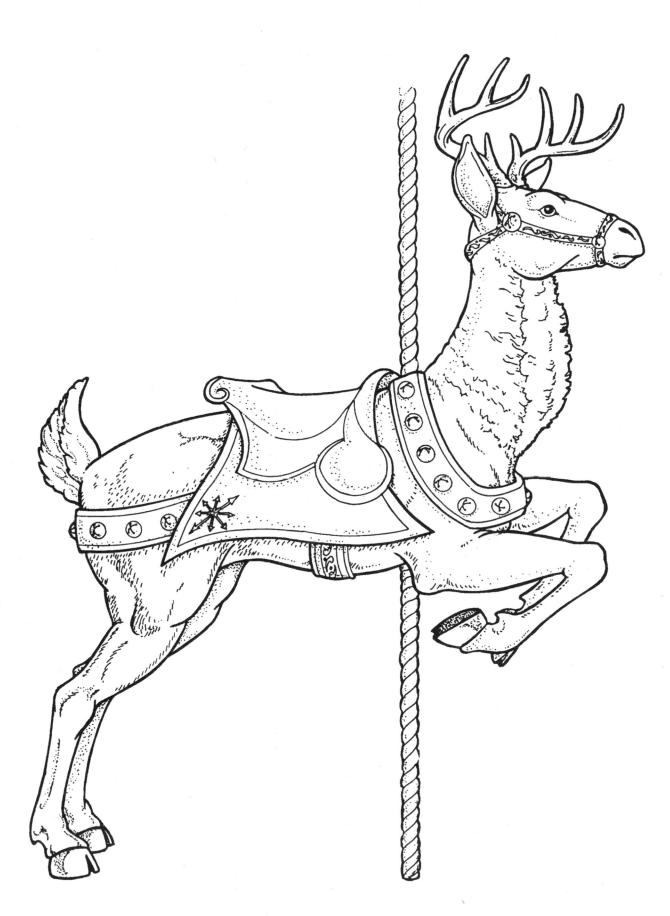

The carver Dentzel often embellished his prancing white-tailed deer with antlers shed by live deer. Since they were more durable than wood, and were readily available, authentic antlers provided a practical alternative to carving. Shown here is a deer drawn in the style of Dentzel.

Carousel carvers created a wide range of whimsical animals. Dentzel-type hares, or rabbits, were generally inner-row jumpers. These gentle giants were often favored by young riders.

The only carousel animals known to wear clothing were frogs created by the Herschell-Spillman Company. These outfits may have been inspired by the classic children's book, *Wind in the Willows*. The frog depicted here is drawn in the Herschell-Spillman style.

Among the most popular of non-equine carousel creatures was the cat. This Dentzel-inspired feline has a fish in its mouth. Additional prey for carousel cats included crabs and ducks.

The sea horses of Neptune, god of the sea, had the heads and forequarters of horses, combined with the tails of dolphins. They were known for pulling Neptune's underwater chariot.

Possibly influenced by tales of the Loch Ness monster, E. Joy Morris created unusual carousel sea creatures much like the one shown in this drawing. Little is known of Morris, an eccentric carver, who created less than two dozen carousels.

Carousel chariots, or benches, are often adorned with beautifully carved sideboards. The one shown here is decorated with dragons. Because they are low to the carousel floor, benches are favored by people too young or too old to climb atop a tall, wooden animal.

Embellish this pony with your own whimsical trappings
to create a unique carousel animal.